HEALING TRUTHS

HEALING TRUTHS

Ten Truths
that Lead to Joy,
Well-being,
and Wisdom

Anne P. Serdula

ENHEART
PUBLISHING
http://www.enheartpublishing.com

P.O. Box 620086
Charlotte, NC 28262

Healing Truths

ISBN 0-965-4899-5-7

Library of Congress Control Number: 2004115004

Book layout by: Dan Robinson
Cover design by: Leah Ponds
Original cover art by: Rosalie Caruso
Printed in the United States of America by Jostens, Charlotte, NC

Acknowledgments

I feel very blessed to be able to share this personal healing journey. I am grateful for all the people who have been in my life at one time or another. I would like to take this time to thank the people who made this book possible.

First and foremost, I thank my mom for giving birth to me and I thank God for my life.

I want to thank my publisher, Pat Schulz, for her knowledge and skill in the publishing business and for making this project come to fruition.

Thank you, Michelle Pratt, for editing this manuscript. I appreciate all of your effort and knowledge of words and writing. You made my story concise and complete.

A special thank you to Ron and Lavana Rathbun, for taking the time to read and endorse this book. Your encouraging words meant the world to me.

I am so grateful and would like to thank my personal healer, Neil Weinberg, for helping me heal throughout the years by unblocking my chi, thus allowing it to flow freely to enhance my personal healing.

My biggest fear when I moved from upstate New York to North Carolina was that I would not find another great acupuncturist. Thank you God, for providing me with another great healer, Dr. Michele Blitstein. Your healing hands and skills in this holistic, complementary modality have helped me remain well, and to flourish in my new environment.

To my grown children, Alysha and Andrew: You both have taught me so much, and have provided me with great strength and encouragement to become a better mom each and every day. I am a student and you are my teachers. Thank you for choosing me to be your mom.

Acknowledgments

For one of my greatest supporters and best girl-friend, Betsy Carlin. Thank you for being there for me throughout the twenty-some years of friendship. Your love and support has helped me believe in myself. I am forever grateful.

And last but not least — to my husband and my best friend, Tony. My life would not be complete without you. I thank you for ALL you do EVERY DAY to make my life so wonderful. Without you, this book would never have been published. Thank you for your belief in me and for your unconditional love and support.

Dedication

This book is dedicated to the love of my life, my husband and best friend, Tony — whose love and support and peaceful state of being has taught and propelled me to realize my own dreams.

Table of Contents

"Blessed is he who finds himself

and wishes to share

what is found with the world."

— Ron Rathbun

Introduction

I have awakened my mind
To hear the spirit within.
I hear its voice as it tries to calm my fears.

Going within on this journey —
Mindfulness, consciousness

The spirit is found.

Thank you God for this wonderful gift!

My intention in writing this book is to help others who are experiencing stress, illness, or difficulty. I want them to know there is a way to find inner peace and joy, no matter what circumstance they are facing. I have finally found inner peace and desire to share what I have learned with anyone struggling with life issues. Inner peace is not a part of the personality. It is that of the soul. I became aware of this way of thinking in order for a transformation and healing to occur in my life.

My journey started years ago when I observed my husband's state of being. I remember often asking him, "How can you be so calm? Don't you feel nervous inside?" He would answer, "No, this is just how I am." I always wanted to be that way. I wanted to experience the sense of inner peace he appeared to possess. Back in our early years of marriage, I started to read self-help books, but I never really understood how to create the change in myself. I now understand that I was not ready to undertake the work required to create this inner change.

As a result, I continued to live as I always had — by my personality — strong, controlling, anxious and stressed.

At a very stressful time in my life, I decided I'd had enough. Everyday I woke up anxious, with headaches and a feeling of dread.

One morning after having a hysterectomy I thought — "What can I do to help myself heal? How can I change to a healthier way of thinking and being?" I knew that if I didn't change my thinking, the emotions that caused my female problems would eventually attack other areas of my body and create ill health — Then what organs would need surgery? I started to educate myself on energy medicine, spiritual healing, and holistic health. I read everything I could get my hands on, listened to wonderful enlightening tapes, and researched the subject non-stop. I learned many healing and transformational ways to create health and a sense of well-being. However, I knew that if I didn't put my newfound knowledge into action it wouldn't help.

Shortly after my self-study began, Oprah started her *Change Your Life* TV series on self-discovery, with wonderful guests like Gary Zukav, Caroline Myss, Iyanla Vanzant, and Dr. Phil McGraw, to name a few. Each one spoke to me loudly and clearly. The teachers appeared when I, the student, was ready!! Little by little I started making changes in my thought patterns and belief system that brought me to an inner peace that I had read about, but never experienced. I finally found the calm within; the inner peace that can transcend any situation. It is a state of joy.

Joy is the inner peace you experience that is of Divine origin. It is a spiritually grounded state of be-ing that exists regardless of the circumstances you are facing. Joy enables you to deal with every situation you face. In the state of joy, you know that all things work out. Joy is that inner peace that you can go to anytime, any place, and under any circumstance.

I found that in order to experience this peace, I had to make a paradigm shift and learn how to see life from my soul's perspective, not from my ego or personality. Many of us have been taught from birth that it is okay to live from our ego. We react to the external world of chaos by taking on the role of victim and by living life externally and materialistically. We have not been taught that *we are more energy than matter.* This energy is the soul within each and every one of us. We must learn how to change our reactions to see from our soul's perspective.

Once you can incorporate these Healing Truths into your life, you will experience how wonderful life becomes. You will handle all situations in a much healthier way.

Remember, it will take a conscious effort on your part to do the inner work required. These Healing Truths, when applied to your mindset, will transform you from the inside out — allowing you to live your best life — one of contentment, inner peace and joy.

"*It is the attempt that brings
about the trying.
It is the trying that brings
about the doing.
And it is the doing that
brings about the being.*"

— Ron Rathbun

Healing Truth Number One

Life is Full of Lessons

You can either choose to
learn from the
lessons & grow in wisdom,
Or you can choose to ignore the lessons & experience
stress & pain.

Which do you choose?

As an adult, I realized every experience in life is a lesson. We can either ignore the lesson, or use it to gain great wisdom. The purpose of life is to grow in wisdom and love. Once you accept this truth — life is a fun adventure, not something to dread and to just *get through.*

Lessons come in all sorts of sizes and packages. Divorce, the loss of a loved one, betrayal, or even lawsuits are all examples of situations that are full of lessons you may need to experience in order to grow. One lesson is not necessarily more important than another. Lessons can be found when a car cuts you off on the road, or when an angry person screams at you. Knowing that all events are meant to teach us something — they are not random — helps us accept and deal with stressful situations. *Know that all things are happening for a reason.* The reason is to help you grow spiritually into the person you are meant to be.

The key point to remember is that it is *your reaction* to a situation that helps you either remain calm or stimulate stress. Once you become mindful, or aware of how you are choosing to react to circumstances, you will find life and its difficulties are much easier to handle.

It is important to know that each of us has to learn our own lessons in life. We cannot learn lessons for another person, and we cannot force them to learn lessons that will help them change. We are here to work on our own lessons.

Changing how you think can greatly alter a situation. The word *problem* has a negative connotation; therefore, just by changing the word *problem* to *opportunity,* you create a feeling of challenge instead of something to dread. It puts you in charge of the situation. This is a simple example of how changing your mind can change your life and ultimately how you view the world.

I was brought up in a family that always over-reacted on an emotional level. Anxiety was the norm, and as an adult I followed the pattern that was set in my childhood. I am not blaming my parents for my state of being; I am simply acknowledging where my destructive behavioral patterns originated. As an adult I realized the old patterns were not working for me. It was up to me to change them and develop new ones that were healthy and constructive. It is unproductive and destructive to blame your parents — as hard as it may be — you must accept they did the best they could with the knowledge they had at that time.

I have experienced many hard lessons, but I know they all happened to bring this wonderful inner growth. I could not have developed fully without each experience. I am thankful for all of my lessons.

One of the harder lessons in my life was when my husband filed for bankruptcy. I became the target of a lawsuit. At first I had a difficult time comprehending how this could be happening to me. I took on the role of victim and started blaming other people for what was happening to me. I started to panic, and I suffered from severe anxiety. I could not bring myself to a state of calm, because I had never experienced it before. At one point I needed medicine to help me cope. I knew I needed help. I needed to learn a whole new way of thinking.

Ironically, I see that whole ordeal as a great gift, and I have become very grateful for that opportunity to grow. Bankruptcy enabled me to find my inner strength, my inner peace. When I changed the way I thought about the situation, and finally released the need to be in control, I was able to convert from a state of anxiety to a state of calm. I have learned no matter what happens in my life, if I choose to look for the lesson, I can find great wisdom and Truth.

When my daughter was in a very bad motorcycle accident, my state of being was tested everyday. Being three hundred miles away from her added stress and anxiety to an already emotional time. When the phone call came from the hospital to tell us that she had been in an accident and was now in the intensive care unit, I could have lost control. However, I chose to remain calm and deal with the situation with my new way of thinking and being. I chose to apply every Truth I write about in this book. Since these Truths had been ingrained in my mind, they helped me to deal with this serious situation. During my daughter's stay in the hospital intensive care unit, I asked myself, "What is the best way to react to this situation?" The old Anne would have been a wreck — crying and carrying on — but I chose to believe all things would work out according to God's plan, not mine. What would losing control do? It would create a worse situation for myself and for those around me. It would create an environment around my daughter that was not conducive to healing. I chose to remain calm, trust God, and look for the lessons I was supposed to learn. I am not saying this was easy, but it sure beat going crazy.

One day I was not let into the intensive care unit because I was too early and visiting hours had not begun. I woke that morning in my hotel room hearing my daughter calling me. I knew she needed me, so I went over to the hospital and upon reaching the intensive care unit, I was told by the nurses I could not go in as it was too early. Needless to say, I chose to revert back to my old behavior patterns. I cried and carried on — I lost control and consequently I lost my inner peace. It did not do my daughter or me any good. I knew if I wanted to regain inner peace, I needed to meditate, pray and do deep breathing exercises. It worked! What a great lesson.

I realized on this journey of self-discovery and

healing that it was *my reaction* to the situation that could make my life either more tranquil or more stressful. Once I understood that my response determines my inner peace and that everything happens for a reason — it was easier to give up my over-reactions. If I wanted to live in peace I needed to change my thinking and my reactions.

In retrospect, I see every crisis I have gone through with each of my children as a gift, because every encounter has been an opportunity for us to grow. Where would we be without these lessons?

We need to learn everyday — otherwise we become stagnant and die. Each and every day holds many new lessons and adventures. Life is for the living — don't let it pass you by. Get out and do the things you want to do today, because tomorrow may never arrive. Live your life to the fullest, and take time every day to reflect on the lessons you have learned.

Why not take this opportunity to expand your mind, your body and your soul? Believe there are no mistakes, only lessons to be learned. Change your thinking to incorporate this Truth.

"If you don't like something, change it.

If you can't change it,
change the way you
think about it."

Healing Truth Number Two

Live From Your Soul

Often wondering why I am here...
I found the answer by going within myself —
To the deepest level of my soul;
My spirit.

What a wonderful life it is now to live —
once having awakened the spirit.

Each one of us has a soul: the power of God within. We are all filled with this universal energy. It is the life force. The Chinese refer to this force as "Qi," the Hindu's as "Prana." We are energy that continually flows from our feet to our head and from our head to our feet. The energy in us is of Divine origin.

To transform your life, you need to react to life's situations with your soul, and not with your ego. This connection with your soul is vital if you truly want to change your life. Start to think of yourself as a soul with a personality. Become one with your soul, and choose the life of inner peace and joy.

Our ego does not allow us to love. It is based and formed on fear. Our soul, on the other hand, is of the Divine. *It is love.* The ego cannot let go of fear. It wants to be in control. It reacts in ways that are negative or un-loving. The ego reacts through our personality, not our soul. Responding from the soul is responding from love.

It means trusting God — something our ego cannot do.

Awareness is the key to change. Awareness is your key to success. If you are not aware, how can you change? Awareness allows you to take action, to stop blaming other people, and to claim responsibility for your life. Choosing awareness allows you to think from your soul. You will reap the rewards of compassion and understanding from thinking on this level. Becoming aware of your soul within will transform your life. Responding from the soul is not an easy task. It takes constant work. It is a process, not an end result. It is during this process that we create positive change within ourselves.

The Truths in this book are that of the soul. When we start to react to life from our soul, life becomes less stressful, and easier to manage. It is necessary to train yourself to react from this soul level. At first we may not like this change, but it is vital to incorporate these truths into our behavior in order to bring about positive and healthy changes.

Profound awareness came into my life when I began to understand energy and energy medicine. I realized feelings of anger and resentment were depleting my body of the energy I needed to maintain my health and well-being. I realized every thought, every word and every action had a direct consequence on my cells, which had a direct effect on my immune system and therefore my health. Once I understood and accepted this, I wanted to keep my energy positive, strong and healthy. I wanted to keep this energy inside of me to maintain my health. I became selective with releasing my energy. I would think, "How would I react to this situation from my soul?" or "Do I want my energy to leave my body in the form of anger or resentment?" I had to incorporate this wonderful soul-level thinking into my thought patterns.

This truth can transform your life if you let it take hold of your mind. Responding to life from your soul will set you free. It will relieve you of your negative reactions to other people and to life's circumstances. By becoming aware of how you are reacting and choosing to respond from your soul, you will deal with all areas of your life in a much healthier way. Realize that you are a soul in a body and that you can start to act from this soul level instead of from your ego. Choose soul level reactions and you will grow in wisdom.

"The beauty of the day is contingent
upon your seeing it."

— Ron Rathbun

Healing Truth Number Three

Live in the Present Time

*Take time to bring your mind and thoughts
to the present moment.
Healing and joy can only exist
in the present time.*

In order for joy and healing to occur it is necessary to incorporate this Truth — Live in present time. What are you thinking about as you read these words? Are you thinking about the argument you had with your friend? Are you thinking about your job interview tomorrow? If you are, you are not living in present time. You are thinking of an event in your past or of one in your future. In order to experience joy, it is necessary to bring yourself back to the present time — the moment of now.

The present time is this very moment. Reading these words right now is living in present time. Your attention is in tune with your reading, absorbing this information. Today is present time — not tomorrow or yesterday. Bringing your awareness to present time makes you conscious of all that is happening. It allows you to feel grateful for this precious moment.

Keeping your awareness in present time will

help alleviate worries. Worries do not exist in the present. Realize that whenever you start to worry, you are no longer in the here and now; you are in the *what if.* You are thinking of something that *might* happen. If you worry, will it change the future? Of course not. You worry when you feel you need to control the situation. Accept that *you are not in control!* You can't control what is happening, but you can control your thinking. When you worry, you are thinking in the future tense and you lose vital energy. Worry and anxiety can deplete your energy to the point of making you ill. In order to stop feeling anxious, it is necessary to bring your thoughts back to present time by repeating the phrase, "All I have is now," or "Live in present time." Repeat this phrase until it resonates within every cell of your body. Realize that the present time is all you have. Your soul is a present time creature. It cannot live in the future nor in the past without depleting energy from your body.

When you start to ruminate over the past, you are no longer in the present time; you are in the past. The past is over. Leave it there. Don't keep reliving it. There is no way to change what has happened. Your vital energy leaves your body when you are living in the past. You deplete yourself of the energy needed to maintain health and well-being.

Many of us keep thinking of the past events in our life, especially the negative ones, when we were hurt on some level. In order to transform your thinking and your life, you will have to let go of the hurt from events in your past. Of course you will have a very difficult time releasing the pain — but it is the only way for spiritual growth. Bless all the people and all the events in your life. Thank God for all that is. After all, you wouldn't be here today working on your spiritual growth if these things did not happen to you.

When we think we cannot let go of our past, or

when we think we need to keep focusing on our future, we are responding from our ego. However, by living in the present moment, we respond from the soul and we can heal in remarkable ways. Remember, our souls only live in present time and by aligning with our soul, we can experience peace and joy.

Forgiveness is easier when you live in present time, because whatever it is that you need to forgive happened in the past. It did not happen in this present moment — therefore it doesn't exist. We may feel pain and want to hold on to these negative emotions, but it is vital to release this pain and concentrate on the here and now. It is not simple to do, but with conscious awareness and effort on your part, you can transform your thinking and begin to live in the present more often than where you used to live — the past and future.

In applying this lesson, I have been able to break the cycle of anxiety and worry. Bringing myself back to present time when I begin to feel anxious has helped me to focus on the here and now, not on the what might be or what might have been. It helped me find inner peace and joy.

You too can live in the present time. You too can focus on the now. This will allow you to have all the energy you need to heal yourself, to work on issues, or to just be. The soul only knows the NOW — so bring your thoughts back to the present time. Joy can be experienced only in the present time. Focusing on the past or on the future takes your joy away. Working on this lesson can heal your heart and bring immense joy.

"*When you reach your
hand to another;
do so with love.
It will rarely be refused.*"

— Ron Rathbun

Healing Truth Number Four

Live Life Through Love and Forgiveness

Love – The true power of God

(My son refers to this as "Mom's hippie garbage")

Remember the saying, "God is Love?" What does that really mean? If God is love, then love is a Divine emotion. Therefore, we need to come from the energy of love in all that we do. Any emotional response not coming from love is coming from fear. Fear and love cannot exist at the same time. If you are in fear — love is no longer present.

Once you become conscious of this truth, and accept it as true, you will be able to recognize if you are responding from love or from fear. How will you know if you are coming from love or fear? If you choose to respond in anger, you are reacting out of fear. Anger is fear-based. Fear of not being good enough, fear to live the life you really want, fear your kids won't do the right thing. Fear excludes God. When someone upsets you, you may want to respond in anger, but choose from the soul. Love is the emotion of God and you will be more at peace, happier and healthier if you react through love, not fear. Take time to recognize how you respond.

Don't give away your energy in the form of anger. Remember, you need all your energy to remain healthy. It is also necessary to understand the laws of cause and effect. That is what is known as karma. If you decide to respond in anger instead of love, know that the effect of the anger will come back to you in some form. Do you really want to suffer the consequence of this choice? That is why it is so important to respond with love. What goes around does come around.

Responding from love is not always easy. Many things will test our decision throughout each day. However, when we make a conscious effort to react from love we will be acting from our soul, not our ego. This produces growth. The rewards of responding with love are inner strength and peace.

For most of my life, I reacted out of fear, trying to control my life and the people around me. I became angry and swore in frustrating situations. I was reacting out of fear. Fear of thinking I was not good enough, fear of rejection or fear of the unknown. Things changed drastically when I became aware that love is the true power of God, and incorporated this truth into my life. When I could react in a loving way instead of choosing to get upset or angry, I felt at peace. I felt triumphant. I am not saying this is easy, I am saying it is possible. I started to pray for people who I felt had harmed or offended me and offered them love and blessings instead of anger and I experienced the consequences of responding in love. My heart began to fill and I had more love to give.

Love also means being kind and loving to yourself. Love yourself enough to do the right thing. Love yourself and accept yourself for who you are and for all your failings. Whenever you are in any situation that provokes feelings other than love, remind yourself of

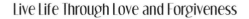

this truth. God is Love and love is Divine power. It will help you center yourself and find peace.

Remember, the goal is to react from your soul and in order to do this you need to respond from love and no longer from your ego with anger and fear.

Forgiveness --
An Act of Self Love

Whom do you hurt when you refuse to forgive someone? The answer is YOU!! You may think by refusing to forgive and by holding back love that you are hurting the other person, but the person you are really harming is you. In order to experience joy, you need to choose the love in your heart and forgive those who have offended you. When you hold on to anger or a grudge, you obstruct the energy flow of love from your heart. The act of forgiveness allows your heart to open wide so the energy of love can begin to flow from your heart throughout your entire body. Forgiveness occurs when the energy of the heart and mind connect. The mind and the body are in conflict when we do not forgive. This affects every cell in your body, creating a situation for illness to manifest. The mind must choose to forgive, and once the choice is made to forgive, the burden of not forgiving will leave the heart. Only then can the energy begin to flow freely. Your heart can be open to give and receive love.

You can forgive another person even without his or her accepting your forgiveness. The person you forgive does not even need to be aware of your forgiveness. This is a personal healing choice you are making and when you forgive, your heart opens and releases the burden. You have opened up your heart and initiated this wonderful state.

This is one of the most difficult steps to take on the journey to inner peace and wellness. Most people can recall a situation that fills them with anger and bitterness or they know of someone who they have not forgiven. *Remember, when you refuse to forgive, you are hurting only yourself.* You are locking yourself up in a prison of anger and pain. You are building a wall around your heart and obstructing the energy flow. This is so un-healthy, and it shields you from being the loving person God created you to be.

Forgiveness unlocks this block. Forgiveness is a choice you make. It is taking a stand and proclaiming that you will not allow yourself to live in this prison of anger and pain any longer.

When you forgive you are releasing yourself from the bondage of holding onto this pain. *Forgiveness is about you, not about another person.* The key is to release the pain and blocked energy around your heart, which allows you to be healed.

It took me a long time to make the choice to forgive. I spent months thinking of all the reasons I shouldn't have to forgive. But in the end, I wanted to do what was best for *me* and I found just by choosing one act of forgiveness, I had set the energy in motion for more forgiveness to follow.

I can recall a particular incident when I needed to forgive a man who created what I felt was unnecessary pain and conflict in my life. The act of forgiveness required baby steps at first. Initially I told myself I had forgiven him, but at the time, I could not feel it in my heart. I prayed that God's love would come into this man's heart. I repeated those words over and over, week after week, and month after month. I could feel my heart accept this and my feelings of anger started to dissolve. Once I realized I was only hurting myself by carrying this anger in my heart toward him, it was much easier to let go and forgive.

Forgiveness does not mean forgetting the incident occurred. It means that when you talk about the incident you don't experience strong feelings of anger and pain. You can actually talk about the past event without feeling negative emotions for the other person. This is how you know that you have truly forgiven someone.

Choose forgiveness and love. Live from your soul, not your ego, for the ego has a hard time forgiving, but our soul *knows only* forgiveness!

*"Give yourself the gift of love
and no other
gift is needed."*

— Ron Rathbun

Healing Truth Number Five

Love and Honor Yourself

*Learning to love yourself
is the greatest love of all,
For you cannot truly love
someone else
If you do not love yourself.*

It is necessary to love yourself before you can ever truly love another. It is the key to spiritual growth. Honoring yourself means living by the principles of integrity and honesty. These principles include truthfulness, commitment, serenity and growth.

Honoring yourself means keeping a commitment to yourself. Are you trying to lose weight and finding it difficult to resist that piece of cake or difficult to stick with your exercise regimen? When you experience moments like these, realize that you honor yourself when you follow through with your commitment. You honor your mind, body and spirit when you eat nutritiously and exercise. Remember that your body is the temple of your soul. Taking care of it is essential, because when your body is functioning well, it gives energy to your mind and strengthens the soul. Rest and relaxation are also ways to honor yourself. Proper rest allows time for the body and mind to rejuvenate. Honor your commitments to yourself and others. Doing so creates a healthy body and a healthy mind.

Truthfulness is vital to your integrity. Speaking truthfully and not maliciously is also a way of honoring yourself and responding from your soul. Setting time aside each day for prayer and meditation gives you the strength to choose honor and integrity.

Gardening, daily walks or doing other things you love are ways to honor yourself. In doing what we love we are living in the present moment, replenishing ourselves and nourishing our soul in order to have enough energy to nourish other people.

It is also necessary to challenge yourself. Challenging your mind and body are necessary for personal growth. It helps you believe in yourself and to gain confidence. We need to live life to the fullest and to our fullest potential. In challenging ourselves, we honor the Divine within because we are responding from the soul by using our body, mind and spirit to reach our highest potential. We are using our minds to grow in knowledge and wisdom. Challenging our physical bodies creates health and well-being, which also honors ourselves.

What a healing truth this is! I have established my inner honor code: what I will allow myself to do and what I will not allow myself to do. I have found numerous ways to honor myself and have finally come to love myself for the first time in my life. I take time to meditate, pray, walk everyday, eat well, and educate myself about various topics. Being truthful with myself and with others is also part of this honor code, as well as thinking positive thoughts about myself. Living by my honor code challenges me to do and be my best at all times.

It is vital for personal growth to take time throughout the day to become aware of your self-talk. Are there positive thoughts ruminating in your mind? Listen frequently to what you are thinking and see if it is beneficial. If you are criticizing yourself — STOP! Negative self-talk creates negatives effects in the body. The mind and the body are one entity. Neuroscientist, Candice Pert, in her book, *Your Body is Your Unconscious Mind*, states there is no separation between the body and mind. Each thought creates a physiologic response and the body releases chemicals and hormones that correlate with that thought. This creates either a negative or a positive effect in the body. Start to say positive things about you to yourself. When you find you are judging yourself harshly, begin to repeat positive affirmations. You honor yourself when you become aware of your self-talk, when you listen to the messages you are affirming in your mind and when you adjust your negative thoughts to positive ones.

Learning to love yourself and living with honor and integrity gives you the freedom to expand your joy for when you honor yourself, you honor the Divine within.

"Love your neighbor
as yourself"

— The Ten Commandments

Healing Truth Number Six

Honor One Another

"Do unto others
as you would have them do unto you."

— *Luke 6:31, The Gospels*

Once you have begun to love and honor yourself, you are ready to love and honor other people. The statement honor one another is self-explanatory. When you honor people you are honoring the Divine in the other person. In yoga, we greet one another with the term Namasté. It means to honor the Divine within the other person. What a beautiful gesture of greeting.

To honor one another means to treat them with respect and dignity. The Bible verse, "Do unto others as you would have them do unto you," is a perfect standard of how to treat other people.

Many times in life we question if we have the strength to choose honor and respect. Remember, *what we do to others will eventually come back to us.* Our world becomes much more peaceful and loving when we start to treat people as we would want to be treated.

Treat people with respect because you want to be treated with respect. Treat people with love because you want to be loved. Treat others with compassion because you want to be treated with compassion.

When you honor people you live by the emotion of love, not fear. Even if someone treats you poorly, choose to respond with honor. Respond from your soul-level of love instead of responding in anger. Know that everyone is just like you: Each person deserves to be treated with honor and love. We are all of God's Divine energy and love needs to be the only way to respond.

"He who separates himself,
Separates himself from all
that is."

— Ron Rathbun

Healing Truth Number Seven

We Are All One With God

*One universal life force flows
through all that is.
We are not separate
from God or from others.*

Have you ever felt the connection to all that is? It is extremely peaceful, to know the profound and powerful truth that we are all connected. We are all made from the one universal life force — God — and this life force runs through each and every one of us, and through all that is. Not only are we all connected, we are also connected to everything in the universe: the animals, the environment and all of nature. Take a deep breath and let this truth resonate within your soul.

We know this truth deep within our soul, for we are born knowing. When we were children we knew this was Truth. It wasn't until we started to grow that we learned that we were different and started to separate ourselves from others. We were taught to believe we were better than other people based on ethnicity or religion.

Some of us heard, "White people are superior to Black people," "Jews are better than Catholics," and these biased thoughts were passed on to us from adults. These messages break our connection and separate us from one another. It is a *learned separation* — a separation from one another, and thus, a separation from God.

Accepting our universal connection makes life easier to live. It brings harmony to your life and a feeling of closeness to all. Once you accept this truth into your life, your life will never be the same. You will start to see people of different races, nationalities, religions, and income levels in a different light. They are the same as you. Your ego may perceive that you are better than someone else. — Remind yourself of this connection whenever you feel superior or inferior to someone else.

If we are all one, how can there be prejudice? If we are all one, how can we continue to destroy our environment, destroy the rain forests, pollute the air, water and earth? How can we harm anything?

Since God created all that is, and God's energy is in all of us and in all that is, how can there be war? How can there be anything but love? Because we think we are separated from one another. We are not! Each one of us is a microcosm in this macrocosm of our universe. Start to make this truth a reality in your life.

We are all connected by the universal life force of God. We are all brothers and sisters. Whatever happens to one of us, happens to all of us. If something terrible happens to our earth, it will affect *all* of us. Although it may not be in our back yard — *it is* going to affect all of mankind. When all people start to truly believe this Truth — the world will be peaceful and harmonious.

When we accept that all things are connected, we want to love, help and accept all people. Believing this changes our personality and causes us to view all of life as special and unique. We have a peaceful heart. We feel compassion. We want to save our planet from destruction. We want to become active participants in environmental and human rights issues. We want to protect all species, because we understand that they all possess the life force of God.

The next time you hear someone speak ill of a specific race, religion or person — enlighten his or her mind by reminding him or her of the truth — we are all one. We are all the same in the eyes of God.

Serenity Prayer

*"God grant me the serenity
To accept the things I cannot change,
Courage to change the things I can,
And wisdom to know the difference."*

Healing Truth Number Eight

Surrender Your Will

Release the need to be in control,
for it is in the releasing that we find inner peace,
contentment and God's support.

Surrendering your will to God produces a great feeling of calm and peace because you release your will and allow the will of God to take over your life. You understand that you are not in control — God is! This produces a sense of relief. You are not responsible for the outcome, only your response. By accepting that God is in control, and putting your faith and trust in Him, you release the burden of being in control of every situation. You lighten the load you have to bear. Surrender your will to God means to release the need to control life and let God be in charge, knowing that God knows what's best for us and what is necessary for our spiritual growth. Surrender your will means knowing that whatever happens is meant to happen — whether we want it to or not. Life will not necessarily go the way we would like, or come in the packaging that we may want. We must learn to give our will to God at all times, not just when we experience difficulty. Know that all things are happening for a divine purpose, no matter how difficult it seems.

We will face many situations in life that we know we cannot handle alone. When we trust God to carry the burden, we release our need to control and we lighten our heart. We do this by letting go of the fear, anxiety, and depression. Releasing your will to God requires great trust and faith in the higher power. In our society each person works to become independent in order to feel in control of his or her own life. This is our ego, not our soul. It is a very difficult task to surrender your will and allow God's will to take over, but for spiritual growth, we must surrender our will and allow life to unfold as it is supposed to. Have faith that God knows what is best for our spiritual growth. This occurs on the soul level.

Synchronistic events start to occur with the release of your will, things that others may refer to as coincidence. There is no such thing as coincidence. Whatever happens is supposed to have happened. The universal life force looks out for us and as we co-create or shape our life to this life force, synchronistic events occur for our growth. Things become aligned in the universe to help us achieve what is necessary for growth.

Admittedly, releasing my will to that of God has been difficult, but it is not impossible. My personality, wants to think I am in charge. After many years, I've realized this thought process does not work for me, I released my will and I let God's will be done. When I become frustrated with my children, lawyers, doctors or whomever, many times I chose to release my will to allow the will of God to manifest. — All things did work out, maybe not as I would have planned, but I trust that God knows what is best for me.

"Gratitude is like a magnet
that attracts more of it to itself;
The more grateful you are,
The more you will receive
to be grateful for."

— Iyanla Vanzant

Healing Truth Number Nine

Live with Gratitude

My mind is conscious.
My body is alert.
My spirit is present.
Living life in the conscious state,
Full of positive energy and love.
I thank God for this awakening.
I look forward to every day.
For this I am so grateful.

— Namasté.

Be grateful for all that is: every situation, both good and bad. As Oprah Winfrey wrote in O Magazine*, "It's not easy being grateful all the time. But it's when you feel the least thankful that you are most in need of what gratitude can give you."

By being grateful and concentrating on the good in life, you will start to see even more reasons to be grateful because what you focus and concentrate on draws more of the same to you. Look for the good in life; see the beauty of the things in front of you. Be grateful for small things, such as your breath and large things, such as your family. Feeling grateful can transform your life.

I first learned about gratitude when I read the book, *Simple Abundance* by Sarah Ban Breathnach. I began a gratitude journal as she recommended just to see if it would help me become more content, as she claims. I

---

*Quote from O Magazine, November 2000, Vol. 1, Number 5, Page 298.

started the journal at a time in my life when I was focusing my attention and energy on what was *wrong* in life. This journal was exactly what I needed. It helped me concentrate on the things I was grateful for in my life. Each night I wrote at least five things for which I was grateful. Within a short time, I found many reasons to be grateful. My gratitude grew and grew. When I was in a situation that was troubling, I would give thanks, my troubles would subside, and I would feel less stressed. I chose to see the situation as a lesson to be learned and I received a true blessing and spiritual growth.

I strongly recommend starting your own gratitude journal. Watch your life transform from this simple task. Once you start to cultivate gratitude, your internal world changes, which changes your external world. Care enough about yourself and your well-being to take the time to focus on gratitude.

It is a universal law that we attract to us that

which we concentrate on — so concentrate on being grateful and on giving thanks for the many blessings you receive. Be thankful for all things; remember, look for the lessons to be learned. A simple and wonderful prayer is, "Thank you."

"What you find in your mind
Is what you put there.
Put good things there."

— Ron Rathbun

Healing Truth Number Ten

Develop Wisdom and Nonjudgment

*It takes more than positive
thinking to heal your life.
Wisdom comes from the soul,
Teaching us Truths to live by.*

Wisdom brings clarity and confirms the Truths in this book. Wisdom comes from knowing and accepting that all things happen for a reason. Life's bumps, when looked upon as *lessons and opportunities for growth*, lead to spiritual wisdom. Life suddenly starts to make sense. Wisdom is found within — on the journey of self-discovery or self-study. It is spiritual knowledge that transcends all past beliefs and it allows a person to change his or her beliefs to accept new truths.

When we obtain wisdom, nonjudgment must coincide. In order for spiritual growth to continue, we need to incorporate nonjudgment into our thinking. Realize that when we judge other people, we are creating negative karma for ourselves. When we judge others, we feel we know what's best for them. WE DO NOT! We are not on their journey — for it is their journey, their personal lessons to be learned, and their life to be lived. Therefore, we cannot pass judgment on them. We do not know what lessons they are here to learn.

Nonjudgment must also include the thoughts we have about ourselves. It is harmful to the soul to judge ourselves poorly. Be aware of your inner voice. Are you criticizing yourself? If so, STOP NOW! Our ego judges; our soul does not. Remember, we are trying to grow in wisdom by coming from the soul level, instead of ego. The soul does not judge because *it is wisdom* — it knows that judging will bring negative consequences or karma. Judgment evokes negative feelings and emotions, and it creates negative consequences for us. When we stop judging, we create peace and an open heart so love can flow. It allows us to be compassionate and caring. Stop judging yourself and other people. Judging makes us think we are in control, and that we know what is best for another. Neither of these are true.

We must also release our expectations of other people and of ourselves. Expectations deplete our energy. We cannot avoid feeling disappointment when things do not go the way we planned or hoped — the way we expected.

Depression is a prime example of how expectations can hurt us. We can become depressed when our expectations of life are not being met. In our minds, we have a picture of what we expect our life to be — and when this ideal is not met, it leads to negative self-talk which can lead to depression. In depression we become angry (the anger is turned inward onto the self), instead of taking the necessary steps to create positive change: loving ourselves enough to change those things that are not working.

For me, the task of becoming nonjudgmental continues to be a daily struggle. It continues to be the most difficult truth for me to incorporate into my life. I find myself judging people: believing that I know what's best for them, and what they should do to heal their lives. Since I have become aware of this personality trait, I have begun to recognize when I am judging. I am immediately aware when I pass judgment and I try to make amends right away. I do not want my energy leaving my body in the form of judgment. When I judge, I realize my soul and personality are still not fully aligned. I am thankful that I am aware and conscious of when I am judging others because in the past I was not even aware that I was judging, and I was certainly not aware of the effects of judging. Wisdom comes from knowing this truth.

Wisdom and nonjudgment take a lifetime, or many lifetimes to obtain. The soul brings wisdom and nonjudgment into our lives when we choose to listen and then make a conscious effort to pursue this path. Remember, the soul does not judge.

In life it is important to take an active, responsible role. We cannot blame another person and take on the role of victim if we truly want to be healthy and grow in wisdom. This is why it is necessary to live by these Truths in your life, to change your attitude by responding from your soul, and to create new belief patterns that will assist you in your spiritual growth instead of deterring you from this growth. When you become active you accept the responsibility to create the necessary changes instead of blaming people for your situation. Life is amazing and is very fulfilling when we see from this active, responsible point of view. I encourage each of you to become an active participant in your life — create the life you want to live, the life you were created to live.

Namasté

About the Author

Anne Serdula began her career in the field of nursing. Her passion for health and wellness led her to pursue extensive and in-depth self-study in the field of holistic health and healing.

She is a graduate of Charles S. Wilson Memorial Hospital School of Nursing and Binghamton University, where she earned a degree in Human Development, with an emphasis in Holistic Studies.

Anne resides in Charlotte, North Carolina with her husband Tony. She is an independent Holistic Health Consultant and wellness educator.

To order books or for more information you can visit Anne's website at www.anneserdula.com.

Recommended Reading

One Day My Soul Just Opened Up by Iyanla Vanzant (New York: Fireside Simon & Schuster, Inc. 1998)

The Power Is Within You by Louise L. Hay (Carlsbad, California: Hay House, Inc. 1991)

The Seat of the Soul by Gary Zukav (New York: Fireside Simon & Schuster, Inc. 1989)

The Way Is Within by Ron Rathbun (New York: Berkeley Publishing, Penguin Group. 1994)

Spontaneous Healing by Dr. Andrew Weil (New York: Fawcett Columbine. 1995)

Why People Don't Heal and How They Can by Caroline Myss (New York: Three Rivers Press. 1997)